LONGMAN LITERATURE GUIDELINES

AN INSPECTOR CALLS
J B Priestley

by Theresa Sullivan

Geschenk für den offenen Bücherschrank

Series editors:
John Griffin
Theresa Sullivan

Introduction

One Eva Smith has gone – but there are millions and millions and millions of Eva Smiths and John Smiths still left with us, with their lives, their hopes and fears, their suffering and chance of happiness, all intertwined with our lives, with what we think and say and do. We don't live alone. We are members of one body. We are responsible for each other.

This speech is made by the Inspector near the end of *An Inspector Calls* and perhaps most clearly sums up J. B. Priestley's message. As you read the play, look at the way it unfolds as you begin to realise that every character is implicated in Eva Smith's death. Priestley has constructed his play to point all the time towards this message that we are responsible for each other, a message of particular relevance in Britain today.

It is important that you read, act through or see a production (or film) of *An Inspector Calls* before you begin the work in this book. You will be asked to judge, research, act and draw conclusions. You will be able to study photographs and reviews of performances of the play, and to picture the social world of 1912 that Priestley was recreating. You will also be able to assess the continuing impact of the play: will mankind ever learn to take responsibility for its weaker members?

What is most interesting about the characters in the play is the way that they reveal their true natures under the stress of the Inspector's questioning. The assignments offer you a chance to judge them as characters and to recognise the more selfish and treacherous aspects of human nature.

Contents

The world of *An Inspector Calls* — 4
1912: Arthur Birling's England — 4
People remember — 9
Factory life — 11
Trades unions — 12
Shopwork — 12
Write a speech — 13
Creating a background for the play — 13
Wealth and poverty — 14

Comparisons with other literature — 15
Suffragettes — 15
George Orwell's *Animal Farm* — 17
A more cynical view? — 19
Are these views relevant today? — 19
Charles Dickens' *A Christmas Carol* — 20

Understand the characters — 22
Sheila Birling — 22
Eric's relationship with his parents — 24
Eva Smith — 25
The mysterious Inspector — 25
Mr Birling — 28

Show your understanding of the play's events — 30
Write the scene: Sheila has Eva dismissed — 30
Write the scene: Eva goes to Mrs Birling's committee — 31
Write an interview — 32
Eva Smith's diary — 34
Front page news — 35
The play becomes a novel — 35

An Inspector Calls as theatre — 36
Priestley's advice about writing plays — 36
Staging dramatic moments — 36
Prepare a production — 37
Write a theatre programme — 39
Reviews of various productions — 42

Some advice for coursework — 44
Using quotations in a formal essay — 44
Using quotations in informal work — 45
An entry from Sheila's diary — 45

The world of An Inspector Calls

'We are responsible for each other' is Priestley's clear message in *An Inspector Calls*. In order to demonstrate his message, he sets his play deliberately in 1912, thirty years earlier than the time he was writing. He was writing during the Second World War, when Britain was in a state of upheaval, of a time two years before the outbreak of the First World War. Many people in 1912 were already aware of great changes to come, whereas others, like Mr Birling, thought quite complacently that they had never had it so good.

For many plays and novels, the historical setting may have little relevance, but Priestley's characters are so involved with the social conditions of the time, and Eva Smith is such a vivid example of the fate of many young women living in poverty then, that some understanding of the historical background of the play is necessary.

1912: Arthur Birling's England

Although the whole of the play takes place in the Birling's dining room, we are aware of the outside world, principally through Birling's words, and also through Gerald's and the Inspector's. As the Inspector says to Birling: 'Your daughter isn't living on the moon. She's here in Brumley too.'

Brumley is easily identified as one of the large manufacturing towns of the Midlands. The Birlings are prosperous and live in a fairly large, comfortable house with good solid furniture. Yet a short distance away, but worlds apart in every other way, there are thousands of young women 'counting their pennies in their dingy little back bedrooms'.

When the Royal Exchange Theatre in Manchester put on a recent production of *An Inspector Calls*, a special article was commissioned to relate the social conditions of the time with the play. As you read it, note details which Priestley includes in his play. Then read the comments from people who were actually working in factories and shops during the period from 1880 onwards.

According to the Census of 1911, Arthur Birling's England was a land of some 36 million people. The society they formed was overwhelmingly one of town and city dwellers: nearly 15 million people lived in the great industrial conurbations centred on London, Manchester, Birmingham, Leeds, Liverpool and Newcastle. The heyday of the old, rural England had passed by the start of Queen Victoria's reign in 1837. Farming still accounted for about 1½ million people in 1911, but they amounted to less than ten per cent of the country's work-force. Most people worked in the manufacturing industries, mining, transport and trade, which together accounted for more than two-thirds of the labour force.

The society of Birling's England exhibited huge social divisions and distinctions. Indeed, one historian has observed that 'Class divisions were never so acutely felt as by the Edwardians' (and although King George V was on the throne in 1912, the character of society remained Edwardian).

The most acutely-felt divisions, perhaps, were those of income and wealth, and so of living standards. Calculations based on the tax records for 1911–13 suggest that

87 per cent of the country's total personal wealth – in the form of land and property, bank accounts, stocks and shares, etc. – was concentrated in the hands of a mere five per cent of the population. At the other end of the scale, nearly a third of the country's male manual workers, who with their wives and families added up to something like eight million people, had to get by on less than 25 shillings per week. A contemporary account describes people on that level of income as 'underfed, under-housed and insufficiently clothed . . . Their growth is stunted, their mental powers are cramped, their health is undermined'. And yet, such people were by no means the least fortunate of Arthur Birling's contemporaries.

For most industrial workers, living standards had risen quite considerably in the later years of Queen Victoria's reign. Wages had not gone up much, but prices – especially of everyday items like food and drink – had fallen sharply after 1870. So the money earned went a lot further in 1900 than it had thirty years earlier. (Among the indications of a spreading working-class affluence was the rise of Post Office Savings Bank deposits from £25 million to £135 million between 1875 and 1900, or the pianos (like their owners, upright rather than grand) that had come to grace the parlours of the new artisan suburbs, like Manchester's Hulme.) Along with these economic improvements had gone social, political and environmental changes for the better, in the form of compulsory education, the effective regulation of sanitation and public health, better medical care, the extension of the vote to most of the male population at least, and so on . . . [yet] the social enquirer Seebohm Rowntree reckoned in 1899, for instance, that more than a quarter of the people of York (a city not especially noted for the prevalence of poverty) lived on or below the level of bare subsistence. But things had been getting better in a fairly obvious way for a lot of the Queen's subjects.

But with the turn of the century, the good times seemed to come to an end. Prices rose, and wages hardly kept pace. People who had come to expect steady improvements in their material standards found that prospect now receding, and they resented the fact. There was a heightened awareness, as a result of the work of Rowntree and other investigators, of the continued poverty and the hideous squalor of the city slums. There was a growing dissatisfaction with a system which consigned people after a lifetime of work to the social degradation of the workhouse when they had become too old and frail to support themselves. And there was a growing realisation among working men – thanks, perhaps, to the education they had compulsorily received since 1870, and the political awareness that had come with the vote a few years later – that they had to do something by themselves to remedy these grievances. The appearance of the Labour Party in 1906 and the near doubling of trade union membership between 1900 and 1912 . . . were evidence of the development of an awareness of the distinct identity and interests of the working class and of a determination to push that interest forward by organisation and action.

Meanwhile, businessmen like Arthur Birling were also having an increasingly hard time after 1900. They faced increasing competition, both in their overseas markets and at home, from the rising industrial powers of the USA, Germany, France, Belgium, Russia and Japan. German competition was especially strong, and especially loathed. The fact was that British industry was not always in a good position to meet and beat the competition, even in its own home market.

Its equipment was often less up-to-date and less efficient. Its scale of operations was often smaller, so it could not achieve the same economies as were open to larger American and German firms. Its raw material costs were often higher, and so were its labour costs. Labour costs were particularly important in some of Britain's leading industries: in coal-mining and textiles, for instance, labour accounted for between a half and three quarters of total production costs. Any increase in wages could have a very significant effect on a firm's ability to remain competitive. That is why Arthur Birling was so unwilling to give in to the demand for an increase from his machine operators. He and others like him were becoming increasingly desperate in their efforts to stem the decline in profits . . .

Given the paranoia of industrialists about costs and competition and the resentment of labour about threatened living standards, it hardly comes as a surprise to find that Edwardian England was notable for the growing prevalence of industrial disputes and

the increasing bitterness with which these were contested. Official statistics show that from 1905 to 1909 disputes averaged 456 per year and resulted in an average annual loss of just over four million working days. The figures for 1910 to 1913 show a doubling in the number of disputes and a quadrupling of the working days lost through them. 1912 was a particularly bad year, with the number of working days lost through strikes nearly *ten* times higher than the average for 1905–09. There was an especially prolonged and hard-fought coal strike, supported by the railwaymen and the transport workers who had formed a formidable coalition with the miners known as the Triple Alliance to back each other up in their conflicts with the equally powerful and intransigent coal-owners, railway companies and shipping and stevedoring employers.

Industrial relations was not, however, the only field of serious conflict in Britain in 1912. Since the great Liberal victory in the General Election of 1906, there had been growing conflicts in several other fields which, taken together with the unrest on the industrial scene, generated a rising sense of crisis in the later years of the Edwardian period.

Nor was it just at home that tensions were on the rise and a sense of crisis building up. The same atmosphere seemed to many to pervade the international scene as well. Europe was divided into two hostile alliance systems which ranged France, Russia and Britain against Germany, Austria-Hungary and Italy. Their rivalries over colonies, naval and land forces, spheres of influence and national minorities seemed, to a lot of people, to be leading inexorably to war. Indeed, in 1912 a war had actually broken out in the Balkans as some of the smaller clients of the Great Powers set about carving up the disintegrating Turkish Empire there. Their disagreements about sharing out the spoils, it was feared, could involve the Powers themselves and lead them into a general war.

In Britain, there was a particular belief that it would be necessary, sooner or later, to have a showdown with Kaiser Wilhelm II's Germany, which seemed to threaten Britain's traditional naval and colonial supremacies. By 1912, a, substantial popular literature was in circulation which made Edwardian flesh creep with the prospect of an England invaded and possibly even conquered by Germany, of which the best-known examples were Erskine Childers' novel *The Riddle of the Sands* (1903) and William Le Queux's story of *The Invasion of 1910* (1906). Wide circulation too was given to stories of wild talk in the officers' messes of Wilhelmine Germany, and of toasts to 'Der Tag', the day of reckoning with England. Arthur Birling, as he chats with his son and prospective son-in-law over the port, is inclined to discount all this talk of revolution and war. He believes the country has seen the worst of its internal problems and that despite the rantings of the Kaiser and his wilder officers there is no real threat of war abroad. And he appears to have a special belief in the pacifying effect of technological progress, of motor cars, aeroplanes and ships. Indeed, attitudes like these were by no means uncommon among businessmen like Birling in 1912. They were the heart, for instance, of one of the most popular books of the day, *The Great Illusion* by Norman Angell, which sold over two million copies in the four years following its publication in 1910. Nor were businessmen alone in thinking war improbable: it was a belief they shared with many socialists, among whom it was based on the assumption that working men would recognise war as the highest form of capitalism and would refuse to take part in it. Without them to provide the cannon-fodder, war simply could not take place. There were many people who had to re-evaluate their ideas in August 1914.

Alex Robertson, Department of History, University of Manchester.

People Remember

'It is pathetic, especially on cold, wintry mornings, to note the rivet boys and others of the poorest class as they approach the entrance by the coffee stalls. Their eyes are fixed longingly on the steaming urns and piled-up plates of buns . . . But such luxuries are not for them. They have not a halfpenny in the world, so they content themselves with a covetous look and pass on to the labour . . . All the money is needed elsewhere – for clothes, boots, and household requirements.'

(Alfred Williams, *Life in a Railway Factory*, 1915. The passage refers to the G. W. R. works at Swindon where the author worked for twenty-three years.)

'A family living upon the scale allowed for in this estimate must never spend a penny on a railway fare or omnibus. They must never go into the country unless they walk. They must never purchase a half-penny newspaper or spend a penny to buy a ticket for a popular concert. They must write no letters to absent children, for they cannot afford to pay the postage. They must never contribute anything to their church or chapel, or give any help to a neighbour which costs them money. They cannot save, nor can they join a sick club or Trade Union, because they cannot pay the necessary subscriptions. The children must have no pocket money for dolls, marbles or sweets. The father must smoke no tobacco and must drink no beer. The mother must never buy any pretty clothes for herself or her children . . . Should a child fall ill, it must be attended by the parish doctor; should it die, it must be buried by the parish. Finally, the wage earner must never be absent from his work for a single day.'

'Look at the people who swarm the streets to see the Lord Mayor's Show, and where will you see a more pitiable sight? These beef-eating, port-drinking fellows in Piccadilly, exercised, scrubbed, groomed, they are well enough to be sure; but this other side of the shield is distressing to look at. Poor, stunted, bad complexioned, shabbily dressed, ill-featured are these pork-eating, gin-drinking denizens of the East End. Crowds I have seen in America, in Mexico, and in most of the great cities of Europe . . . Nowhere is there such squalor, such pinching poverty, so many undersized, so many plainly and revoltingly diseased, so much human rottenness as here . . .'

(Price Collier, *England and the English From An American Point of View*, 1909. The author was a visiting American.)

Working conditions were much harder for most people than today. A typical basic working week was about sixty hours – that's eleven hours a day plus a half-day on Saturday. Trade unionism was still in its very early days and workers had very few rights or protection, or control over their working conditions. There were rules and fines in most workplaces for the workers to obey, but few regulations about safety, working conditions and sufficient work breaks. By and large, a worker was at the mercy of his or her employer.

It was estimated in 1899 that for a family of two adults and three children to survive they needed about 21/– a week (£1.05p). On average, men working in towns earned just under a pound, but in the country 15/– (75p) was more common. Women's wages were, on average, half that of men's.

Extracts on this page and on page 10 are from *The Long March of Everyman* edited by Theodore Baker (Penguin).

'There was, I suppose, a great deal of poverty. Naturally, I didn't know much about that as a child. My own dear nurse and the two faithful maids who served us – they never complained of poverty, and when they retired, they were comfortable and had nice places to live, and were always nicely dressed, and could go off for little holidays. It's difficult to know what poverty is.'

(Mrs E. Sillar, BBC Archive Disc.)

'A street of working-class houses ran the length of our garden and we were not allowed to speak, much less play, with the children in this street. On the other side of the house the son of . . . a wealthy Manchester merchant . . . lived with his family. They had a nurse-maid in cap and apron to look after the three children. *They* were not allowed to play with us. We used to stand on the flat top of our summer house and look at both lots of children and say how daft it was that we could not all make up a game of rounders.'

(Davies, *North Country Bred*, 1963.)

Factory life

Factory life was strictly controlled. In 1888 at the Bryant and May match factory in East London, girls were fined out of their week's wages of 4/– (20p) as follows:

> 3d (1½p) for leaving their work area dirty
> 1/– (5p) for putting burnt-out matches on the bench
> 3d (1p) for talking

Other fines commonly imposed in factories were for sneezing: 1d (½p), reading: 1/– (5p), bad language: 1/– (5p), laughing and making a noise: 1d (½p).

Young girls were closely supervised. Flo Mellish remembers:

> 'The first time I ever worked in Fry's, I had to go into a room and learn the way to cover chocolate. And I'm telling you, that was queer. For three days I had someone to teach me. And at the end of that time I had to go on piece work. It was to cover little creams which were called tens. We used to have to cover 120 for three farthings. A couple of weeks after they put it up to a penny. I didn't like it and I didn't get on very well and I really wanted to leave. But of course you couldn't leave. You had to work where you were sent, there was mother at home waiting for the money.
>
> We daren't talk, and we daren't laugh. If we laughed or if we talked we had to leave off. She'd tell you, "Leave off and sit". We had to sit on our stools and wait half an hour. And then we'd start work again. I took home one week 2/10d.'

(Flo Mellish, *Bristol As We Remember It*)

At Courtauld's factory, women employees were dismissed for having an illegitimate child, living with a man unmarried, or bad behaviour at work. The management criticised men for drunkenness and wasting their earnings that should have been spent on their families, but they were not generally dismissed for this behaviour. Courtaulds tried to control all aspects of their women employees' lives; there were classes for them in child care, a lodging house for single girls, and an Amusement Society, which however allowed no drink or music. Attempts were made to influence men's behaviour, but not to the same extent.

Trades unions

By the 1880s workers in unskilled as well as skilled jobs were organising into trades unions in order to improve their wages and working conditions. Although the first trades unions of the 1860s were mostly for men, women in textile factories started forming unions in the 1870s, and the Women's Trade Union League was set up in 1874 to link women's unions on a national basis. In 1888, the 'Match Girls Strike' at Bryant and May was a tremendous victory, because unskilled women workers had taken strike action for the first time, and won their claim for higher wages and better conditions. In 1889 another very important victory was won by the dockers, again an unskilled union, who secured a minimum rate of pay and other improvements in their conditions of work.

In order to get higher wages, male trades unionists often argued that they had wives and children to support. Employers would therefore pay women less and keep them in the lowest-paid jobs. Some male unions adopted the 'middle-class' view that women shouldn't work at all, in order to campaign for a higher 'family wage' for themselves. This attitude was expressed at the 1877 TUC by Harry Broadhurst:

> 'It was their duty as men and husbands to use their utmost efforts to bring about a condition of things where their wives would be in their proper sphere at home instead of being dragged into competition for livelihood against the great and strong men of the world.'

Women trades unionists had a different point of view. They wanted the men's support to get a decent wage for women as well as men:

> 'The real point to be complained of is the low rate of payment earned by the women, and the way to prevent the employment of women in any trade they are unfit for, is for men to join in helping them to combine in order that they may receive the same wages for the same work.'
>
> (Clementina Black, 1887 TUC)

Shopwork

A further opportunity for women at this time was shopwork. Before the 1870s, most shops were family run, for example, the family grocer, selling goods that were packaged on the premises. Any staff employed were men who served an apprenticeship. By 1900, more and more goods were pre-packaged, and the first large stores employing many assistants were opening. Less skill was needed, so apprenticeship declined; the most important aspect of the job was to attract customers. Shop owners started to employ women, especially young and attractive ones, and shopwork gradually became largely women's work, a trend that has continued up to the present day. The job appealed to girls who wanted something a 'cut above' factory work. These were the attractions, according to one writer in 1891:

> 'The work is fairly agreeable, Sundays and evenings are one's own, this to many being an inestimable advantage, and then there is the pleasure of always being able to look nice and neat, also the charm of variety.'
>
> (V. Karsland, *Women and their Work*)

In fact shop assistants had much to complain about. One joke among factory workers was that 'counter jumpers', as they were nicknamed, were paid yearly as their wages were too small to divide by the week. Wages varied from the West End stores in London, who paid their girls £1 per week in the 1880s to local shops paying only 7/- or 8/- (35–40p). Hours varied too, West End stores closing early, while local shops kept their assistants to 11 or 12 o'clock at night. In 1889, one London draper was prosecuted for working two young boys ninety-four hours in one week; he was fined 3/6d (17½p).

One of the worst complaints was that, throughout this long day, assistants were never allowed to sit down, as this was considered a sign of inattentiveness. One London firm provided seats, but told their assistants: 'The young ladies had better not use them if they wish to retain their situations.'

There were often strict rules to follow. Whiteleys, a large London store, had nearly two hundred. Here are some of them:

Shop Rules

Section 14: DISCIPLINE

144. Gossiping, loitering, standing close together, or making unneccessary noise, is Strictly Prohibited.

148. No one to enter or leave business by any other than the appointed doors under pain of dismissal.

151. No Assistant to be insolent to shop walkers or buyers.

154. No young man to have his coat off in the shop while it is open.

155. No Assistant to stand on a chair.

156. No Toilet Business, Nail Cleaning & etc. to be done in the Shops or Showrooms.

Laws passed to regulate hours and conditions of work in shops were slow to take effect, in spite of the unions, and it was not until 1963 that shop workers won the same standards of safety and comfort as factory workers.

Some women were driven to prostitution because of the low wages. In the 1860s, Henry Mayhew interviewed women earning 2½d (1p) per shirt 'finishing' seven shirts a week:

> ' "I went to the streets solely to get a living for myself and my child. If I had been able to get it otherwise I would have done so . . . It was the low price paid for my labour that drove me to prostitution."
>
> She believed that all women in her job were forced into prostitution:
>
> "I never knew one girl in the trade who was virtuous. Most of them wished to be so but were compelled to be otherwise for mere life." '

(Henry Mayhew, *London Labour and the London Poor*)

Write a speech

▷ Imagine that Mr Birling makes a speech to his factory workers during the strike led by Eva. Write his speech, modelling it on the one he makes at his daughter's engagement, and using the article on pages 4–8 to help you. Here are some questions to guide you:

1 How does he justify keeping wages down?
2 What do you think is his attitude towards strikes and strikers?
3 Why does Mr Birling think that war wouldn't happen?

▷ Write the reply Eva Smith, an intelligent woman interested in union affairs, might make. Use these questions to guide you.

1 What would she say about living conditions in England at the time?
2 What would she see as some of the solutions to the poverty and squalor?
3 What would be her attitude towards the strikes?
4 What would be her attitude to families like the Birlings?

Use the comments from people who were actually working in factories and shops during the period (pages 11–13) to help you.

Creating a background for the play

Priestley advised the would-be playwright to: 'Try to suggest life is going on outside your scenes; in poor, thin plays, the characters on stage seem to be the only people left in the world.'

The Inspector says: 'Your daughter isn't living on the moon. She's here in Brumley too.'

▷ Collect quotations from the play which suggest the world of Brumley, a world from which Mr Birling has kept his daughter sheltered.

▷ Imagine that you work in a factory or a shop in Brumley and live alone in poor accommodation. Your family still live a long way off in the country. Write a letter home telling them of your life in Brumley, using as many details as you can from the play. Talk about your feelings about the rich people you have seen in your work.

Wealth and poverty

There are constant references in the play to the wealth, and consequent power and privilege of the Birlings (look at the first five quotations below), and the poverty and powerlessness of Eva Smith (quotations 6 and 7).

1. Tell cook from me. The governor prides himself on being a good judge of port.
2. There's a fair chance that I might find my way into the next Honours List. Just a Knighthood, of course.
3. I was Lord Mayor here two years ago.
4. Well it's my duty to keep labour costs down.
5. This public-school-and-varsity life.
6. He could have kept her on instead of throwing her out. I call it tough luck.
7. She was out of work for the next two months. Both her parents were dead, so that she'd no home to go back to. And she hadn't been able to save much out of what Birling and Company had paid her. So that after two months, with no work, no money coming in, and living in lodgings, with no relatives to help her, few friends, lonely, half-starved, she was feeling desperate.

▷ In groups, search for other references to wealth and poverty.

▷ In pairs, improvise interviews with Mr Birling and then with Eva, in which they are asked about the way they live.

Write up the interviews, using as much of the information you have collected from the quotations as you can.

▷ How has the designer of this production of *An Inspector Calls* tried to suggest the wealth of the Birlings in the set?

Comparisons with other literature

Suffragettes

In 1911, a year before that in which *An Inspector Calls* is set, Gertrude Colmore wrote a novel called *Suffragettes: A Story of Three Women*. She was herself a suffragette and was writing from first hand experience about women's fight for recognition and equality. She chose three women from different backgrounds through whom to tell her story. One woman is from a very privileged and wealthy background who, like Sheila, becomes caught up in the lives of the less fortunate. Another, Sally, is from a background similar to Eva Smith's. She is a maid in a not very well-to-do household, and therefore is at the very bottom of the ladder of employment. In this extract we get a glimpse of the humiliation which she endures because she is not in a position to fight back. She is returning home late after her first suffragette meeting.

A sky, starless and deserted by the moon, mattered little where lamps were frequent and shops poured floods of brightness out on to the pavements; and Sally Simmonds, hastening along Holloway, did not notice that above the street lamps the night hung densely black. She had her two hours out and was hurrying home – that is to say, to the home of her employers – to get the master's supper. She was late, and the master did not like to be kept waiting; nevertheless, though her feet hastened, Sally's mind was not occupied with supper, nor with Joe Whittle, though she had seen Joe that afternoon, though he had put his arm round her waist, and though demonstrative affection was pleasant to Sally. Joe was in the background, dimmer even than the dim presentiment of the master and his supper which loomed upon the outskirts of her consciousness. The forefront of that consciousness was filled with a medley of impressions, new, stimulating; giving rise to all manner of queer sensations and ideas; absorbing her attention, translating her from the humdrum streets into an extraordinary world, dazzling, undreamed of.

Instinctively she hurried, and instinctively she took the right turns to bring her to Brunton Street; but the real Sally was no more in North London than the moon was in the sky. Sally, indeed, was in a sky of her own, and she came down with a sort of flop to sober sordidness when she reached the area gate. How it creaked! No chance of stealing in unnoticed. Mrs. Bilkes would hear her to a dead certainty, and be down upon her with red face and scolding speech. Well, it was worth while if – The back door was opened from within; not the mistress, but the master stood on the other side of it. That was worse in one way, though better in another. The mistress scolded, but the master kissed.

'You're late, my gal. Come in, there's nothing to be afraid of. I ain't hard on you. You've got to pay for keeping a starved man waiting, though. Here now, don't be nasty over it, and I'll swear all I'm worth that the dining-room clock's ten minutes fast.'

The master's arm was round her waist and the master's hard, bristly moustache scraped her cheek. She did not want that encircling arm, and she greatly disliked that particular moustache, yet she accepted the embrace almost without resistance. It was in the day's work, so to speak; most men were like that; most masters, at any rate – in Sally's experience; and it was pretty well a foregone conclusion when she undertook the post of "general" at 9 Brunton Street that Mr. Bilkes would kiss her when Mrs. Bilkes was not looking. She had known it from the look on his face, the particular glint in his eye; having to fight the world "on her own" had made her a judge of faces. As for complaining – the mistress always took the master's side and called you a bad name, and you lost your place for nothing. It was best to keep quiet; and she took what she called "jolly good care" that the unsolicited attentions went no further than an occasional embrace.

So she gave a mental shrug of the shoulders, wiped her cheek when she got into the kitchen, and set the supper to heat. It had been prepared before she went out, and while it was getting hot she took off her jacket and hat, put on a crumpled white apron and a grey-white bow of coarse lace, which did duty as a cap, and went upstairs to lay the cloth.

Mr. Bilkes was lying back in the arm-chair by the fire, absorbed, apparently, in the evening paper. Mrs. Bilkes was sitting by a small side-table, making a blouse. She looked up as Sally came into the room.

'You're late, Sarah. It's past seven now, and the cloth not laid.'

▷ What is Sally's attitude to the Master's intentions? Why does she have this attitude? In what ways is her experience similar to Eva Smith's? What made it possible for women to be treated in this way? Are women still treated like this?

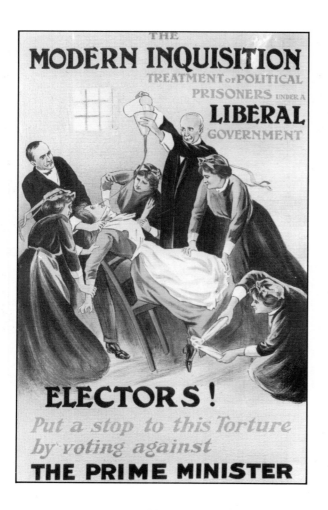

▷ Imagine that it is Eva's first evening at the Palace Variety Theatre bar. She sees the 'hard-eyed dough-faced women' who are used to the place, and men like Old Joe Meggarty 'half-drunk and goggled eyed' who attempts to wedge her into a corner with that 'obscene fat carcase of his'. Write about the occasion and her meeting with Gerald as if it were a short chapter in a novel. Bring out the attitude of the men towards her and hers towards them, as she begins to realise that this is the only way she has left to earn a living.

George Orwell's *Animal Farm*

It is no coincidence that *An Inspector Calls* had its first performance in Moscow, where it was received very well. Priestley never actually uses the word communism – the nearest he comes to it is when he has Mr Birling talk dismissively about it:

... But the way some of these cranks talk and write now, you'd think everybody has to look after everybody else, as if we were all mixed up together like bees in a hive – community and all that nonsense.

Nevertheless Priestley shares the view that communism puts forward. This is what the Inspector says near the end of the play:

We are members of one body. We are responsible for each other.

Animal Farm by George Orwell was published in the same year as *An Inspector Calls*. It opens with Old Major, a prize boar, addressing all the animals on the farm about their miserable brutish lives. As you read his speech, decide how far you think Priestley would agree with him.

'Comrades, you have heard already about the strange dream that I had last night. But I will come to the dream later. I have something else to say first. I do not think, comrades, that I shall be with you for many months longer, and before I die I feel it my duty to pass on to you such wisdom as I have acquired. I have had a long life, I have had much time for thought as I lay alone in my stall, and I think I may say that I understand the nature of life on this earth as well as any animal now living. It is about this that I wish to speak to you.

'Now, comrades, what is the nature of this life of ours? Let us face it: our lives are miserable, laborious, and short. We are born, we are given just so much food as will keep the breath in our bodies, and those of us who are capable of it are forced to work to the last atom of our strength; and the very instant that our usefulness has come to an end we are slaughtered with hideous cruelty. No animal in England knows the meaning of happiness or leisure after he is a year old. No animal in England is free. The life of an animal is misery and slavery: that is the plain truth.

'But is this simply part of the order of nature? Is it because this land of ours is so poor that it cannot afford a decent life to those who dwell upon it? No, comrades, a thousand times no! The soil of England is fertile, its climate is good, it is capable of affording food in abundance to an enormously greater number of animals than now inhabit it. This single farm of ours would support a dozen horses, twenty cows, hundreds of sheep – and all of them living in a comfort and a dignity that are now almost beyond our imagining. Why then do we continue in this miserable condition? Because nearly the whole of the produce of our labour is stolen from us by human beings. There, comrades, is the answer to all our problems. It is summed up in a single word – Man. Man is the only real enemy we have. Remove Man from the scene, and the root cause of hunger and overwork is abolished for ever.

'Man is the only creature that consumes without producing. He does not give milk,

he does not lay eggs, he is too weak to pull the plough, he cannot run fast enough to catch rabbits. Yet he is lord of all the animals. He sets them to work, he gives back to them the bare minimum that will prevent them from starving, and the rest he keeps for himself. Our labour tills the soil, our dung fertilizes it, and yet there is not one of us that owns more than his bare skin. You cows that I see before me, how many thousands of gallons of milk have you given during this last year? And what has happened to that milk which should have been breeding up sturdy calves? Every drop of it has gone down the throats of our enemies. And you hens; how many eggs have you laid this year, and how many of those eggs ever hatched into chickens? The rest have all gone to market to bring in money for Farmer Jones and his men. And you, Clover, where are those four foals you bore, who should have been the support and pleasure of your old age? Each was sold at a year old – you will never see one of them again. In return for your four confinements and all your labour in the field, what have you ever had except your bare rations and a stall?

'And even the miserable lives we lead are not allowed to reach their natural span. For myself I do not grumble, for I am one of the lucky ones. I am twelve years old and have had over four hundred children. Such is the natural life of a pig. But no animal escapes the cruel knife in the end. You young porkers who are sitting in front of me, every one of you will scream your lives out at the block within a year. To that horror we all must come – cows, pigs, hens, sheep, everyone. Even the horses and the dogs have no better fate. You, Boxer, the very day that those great muscles of yours lose their power, Jones will sell you to the knacker, who will cut your throat and boil you down for the fox-hounds. As for the dogs, when they grow old and toothless, Jones ties a brick round their necks and drowns them in the nearest pond.

'Is it not crystal clear, then, comrades, that all the evils of this life of ours spring from the tyranny of human beings? Only get rid of Man, and the produce of our labour would be our own. Almost overnight we could become rich and free. What then must we do? Why, work night and day, body and soul, for the overthrow of the human race! That is my message to you, comrades: Rebellion! I do not know when that Rebellion will come, it might be in a week or in a hundred years, but I know, as surely as I see this straw beneath my feet, that sooner or later justice will be done. Fix your eyes on that, comrades, throughout the short remainder of your lives! And above all, pass on this message of mine to those who come after you, so that future generations shall carry on the struggle until it is victorious.'

▷ Imagine that, while on strike at Birling's factory, Eva makes a speech to her fellow workers about their conditions. Write her speech following the structure of Old Major's speech. Find human equivalents for some of the examples he gives from the animals' lives.

A more cynical view?

Orwell had a perhaps more cynical view of the consequences of communism than Priestley. After the rebellion, the pigs take over the same role as Farmer Jones in keeping the animals in miserable conditions so that they can live well.

▷ Would you agree with Orwell that this is inevitable? Will there always be rich and poor? Is this acceptable if the rich help and take responsibility for the poor? Is there any truth in Birling's idea that, if you look after your own, the world will take care of itself?

Are these views relevant today?

Animal Farm and *An Inspector Calls* were written over forty years ago. Is what they have to say relevant today? Are any of the attitudes still common today? Priestley saw the future optimistically in the hands of young people (Sheila and Eric). Do you think young people of today share Sheila's and Eric's feelings and views?

▷ Imagine that you are a great grandchild of Sheila and that you have found her diary for the year 1912, in which she gives an account of the Inspector's visit. Describe the effect it has on you, so many years later. Do you sympathise with her viewpoint or do you find it strange? Does she seem naive to be so upset over the fate of a factory girl? Or do you think you would feel the same?

Charles Dickens' *A Christmas Carol*

Charles Dickens, writing in the nineteenth century, felt the same concern as Priestley for the poor. He too felt that the rich must take responsibility. Read this extract from *A Christmas Carol* in which Scrooge is asked to give generously to charity.

'Scrooge and Marley's, I believe,' said one of the gentlemen, referring to his list. 'Have I the pleasure of addressing Mr. Scrooge, or Mr. Marley?'

'Mr. Marley has been dead these seven years,' Scrooge replied, 'He died seven years ago, this very night.'

'We have no doubt his liberality is well represented by his surviving partner,' said the gentleman, presenting his credentials.

It certainly was; for they had been two kindred spirits. At the ominous word 'liberality', Scrooge frowned, and shook his head, and handed the credentials back.

'At this festive season of the year, Mr. Scrooge,' said the gentleman, taking up a pen, 'it is more than usually desirable that we should make some slight provision for the Poor and destitute, who suffer greatly at the present time. Many thousands are in want of common necessaries; hundreds of thousands are in want of common comforts, sir.'

'Are there no prisons?' asked Scrooge.

'Plenty of prisons,' said the gentleman, laying down the pen again.

'And the Union workhouses?' demanded Scrooge. 'Are they still in operation?'

'They are. Still,' returned the gentleman, 'I wish I could say they were not.'

'The Treadmill and the Poor Law are in full vigour, then?' said Scrooge.

'Both very busy, sir.'

'Oh! I was afraid, from what you said at first, that something had occurred to stop them in their useful course,' said Scrooge. 'I'm very glad to hear it.'

'Under the impression that they scarcely furnish Christian cheer of mind or body to the multitude,' returned the gentleman, 'a few of us are endeavouring to raise a fund to buy the Poor some meat and drink, and means of warmth. We choose this time, because it is a time, of all others, when Want is keenly felt, and Abundance rejoices. What shall I put you down for?'

'Nothing!' Scrooge replied.

'You wish to be anonymous?'

'I wish to be left alone,' said Scrooge. 'Since you ask me what I wish, gentlemen, that is my answer. I don't make merry myself at Christmas and I can't afford to make idle people merry. I help to support the establishments I have mentioned – they cost enough; and those who are badly off must go there.'

'Many can't go there; and many would rather die.'

'If they would rather die,' said Scrooge, 'they had better do it, and decrease the surplus population. Besides – excuse me – I don't know that.'

'But you might know it,' observed the gentleman.

'It's not my business,' Scrooge returned. 'It's enough for a man to understand his own business, and not to interfere with other people's. Mine occupies me constantly. Good afternoon, gentlemen!'

Seeing clearly that it would be useless to pursue their point, the gentlemen withdraw. Scrooge resumed his labours with an improved opinion of himself, and in a more facetious temper than was usual with him.

Scrooge is visited by the Ghost of Christmas Present.

▷ What similarities and what differences are there between Scrooge and Mr Birling? Scrooge becomes a generous person by the end of the story as a result of three visits by ghosts who point out to him the effects of his meanness and lack of care in a series of dreams. Compare this ending with the ending of *An Inspector Calls*.

▷ Imagine that the dead Eva Smith visits Mr Birling in a dream. What would she say to him? What would she show him?

Understand the characters

In a novel, a writer can *tell* us how a character moves, speaks and thinks. In a play, our only guide to a character is what he or she says. The playwright must be very skilled to create dialogue which reveals character. He or she cannot say that a character is angry, proud, affectionate, happy, miserable or whatever – it must be made clear in the character's words. We need to listen to the words a character is given and decide in what tone of voice they should be spoken.

▷ Look at these photographs of actors taking part in a production of *An Inspector Calls*. Decide which part each actor played. How did you come to your decision?

Sheila Birling

▷ Imagine:
a) that you are a friend of Sheila;
b) that you dislike Sheila.
Write two accounts of Sheila from each of these viewpoints, making sure that in both cases you tell the truth about her. Use these references to help you.

1 So you be careful.

2 But these girls aren't cheap labour – they're *people*.

3 I felt rotten about it at the time and now I feel a lot worse.

4 So I'm really responsible?

5 I caught sight of this girl smiling at Miss Francis – as if to say: 'Doesn't she look awful' – and I was absolutely furious.

6 It was my own fault.

7 Why – you fool – *he knows*.

8 You musn't try to build up a kind of wall between us and that girl. If you do, then the Inspector will just break it down.

9 Well, we didn't think you meant Buckingham Palace.

10 And I'm not a child, don't forget I've a right to know.

11 But this has made a difference. You and I aren't the same people who sat down to dinner here.

12 No, no, please! Not that again. I've imagined it enough already.

13 Mother – stop – stop!

14 I don't care about that. The point is, you don't seem to have learnt anything.

15 And don't let's start dodging and pretending now. Between us we drove that girl to suicide.

16 And it frightens me the way you talk, and I can't listen to any more of it.

17 Not yet. It's too soon, I must think.

▷ Compare these two actresses playing Sheila. What aspects of Sheila's character and feelings is each expressing?

Eric's relationship with his parents

We learn about characters not only from what they say but from what others say about them. Here are two comments from Eric on his parents and the way they brought him up.

. . . you're not the kind of father a chap could go to when he's in trouble – that's why.

You don't understand anything. You never did. You never even tried . . .

▷ What evidence is there in the play that he is right about the way they treat him?

▷ Imagine a quarrel in which Eric accuses his mother of caring about all the wrong things. Write the quarrel in the form of a play.

▷ Imagine that you are Eric and have just found out that Eva Smith is pregnant. He thinks about going to his father for help but then rejects the idea. Write down his thoughts, as you would imagine them to be based on his attitude to and knowledge of his father.

Eva Smith

There is one important character in the play whom we never meet – Eva Smith. Yet we can build up a clear picture of her from what the other characters say. Here is what Mr Birling says: 'lively, good-looking girl'; 'country-bred'; 'good worker'; 'foreman . . . ready to promote her'; 'causing trouble'; 'one of the ringleaders'. Sheila describes her in this way: 'a very pretty girl'; 'big dark eyes'; 'looked as if she could take care of herself'.

▷ Collect similar references to Eva Smith from Gerald, Eric, Mrs Birling and the Inspector.

▷ Imagine that you have been asked to write a report on Eva's character to present at court. You have interviewed each member of the family in order to compile your evidence. Now write your report.

The mysterious Inspector

The Inspector is a mysterious character who enters and leaves the play without any satisfactory explanation. Is he a police inspector? Or is he some supernatural creature as his name suggests?

▷ Study these quotations said by him and about him. What do they reveal about him? Does he sound to you like a police inspector or not? Or are some of the things he says ambiguous, suggestive both of a policeman and of a man who has come in judgment on these people to make them learn from their experience? Use these quotations to help you in your discussion.

1 One person and one line of enquiry at a time. Otherwise there's a muddle.

2 It's my duty to ask questions.

3 I'm not going until I know *all* that happened.

4 It might be you know.

5 You talk as if we were responsible. (Sheila)

6 In fact, I've thought that it would do us all a bit of good if sometimes we tried to put ourselves in the place of these young women counting their pennies in their dingy little back bedrooms.

7 That's more or less what I was thinking earlier tonight . . . A nice little promising life there, I thought, and a nasty mess somebody's made of it.

8 Getting a bit heavy-handed aren't you, Inspector? (Gerald)

9 Why – you fool – *he knows.* Of course he knows. And I hate to think how much he knows that we don't know yet. (Sheila)

10 You see, we have to share something. If there's nothing else, we'll have to share our guilt.

11 You seem to have made a great impression on this child, Inspector. (Mrs Birling)
We often do on the young ones. They're more impressionable. (Inspector)

12 That – I consider – is a trifle impertinent, Inspector. (Mr Birling)

13 You needn't give me any rope. (Inspector)
No, he's giving us rope – so that we'll hang ourselves. (Sheila)

14 Don't stammer and yammer at me man. I'm losing all patience with you people.

15 We don't live alone. We are members of one body. We are responsible for each other. And I tell you that the time will soon come when, if men will not learn that lesson, then they will be taught it in fire and blood and anguish.

16 Then look at the way he talked to me . . . I mean, they don't *talk* like that. (Mr Birling)

17 He wasn't an Inspector. (Mr Birling)
Well, he inspected us all right. (Sheila)

▷ Imagine that each member of the Birling family is asked by a policeman to give their impressions of Inspector Goole. Will each character have a different impression of him? Write down what each would say about Inspector Goole.

▷ Compare these three actors playing Inspector Goole. What aspects of the Inspector's character does each one capture?

Mr Birling

▷ What advice would you give to an actor who is to play Mr Birling about his character and about how he should say his lines? Use these quotations as a basis for your work.

1. As a matter of fact, Finchley told me it's exactly the same port your father gets from him.
2. When Crofts and Birlings are ... working together – for lower costs and higher prices.
3. I speak as a hard-headed business man.
4. Just let me finish, Eric.
5. We hard-headed practical business men.
6. Just a knighthood.
7. You see, I was Lord Mayor here two years ago when Royalty visited us.
8. I don't want to lecture you two young fellows again.
9. I've learnt in the good hard school of experience – that man has to mind his own business and look after himself and his own.
10. If you don't come down sharply on some of these people, they'd soon be asking the earth.
11. Now look here, Inspector.
12. I must say, Sybil, that when this comes out at the inquest, it isn't going to do us much good. The Press might easily take it up.
13. I've got to cover this up as soon as I can.
14. Look, Inspector – I'd give thousands – yes thousands.
15. And really, when I come to think of it, why you all had to go letting everything come out like that, beats me.
16. I'll admit now he gave me a bit of a scare at the time.
17. Nonsense! You'll have a good laugh over it yet.

▷ Compare these two actors playing Mr Birling. What characteristics does each capture? Which one do you prefer? Why?

Show your understanding of the play's events

The work in this section is designed to allow you to show that you have absorbed and understood the events of the play and their implications. It will also allow you to show an awareness of Priestley's style in your responses.

Write the scene: Sheila has Eva dismissed

▷ Write the scene in which Sheila has Eva dismissed from Milwards.

1 Reread pages 22 and 23* of *An Inspector Calls*. Here is a summary of what Sheila says about the incident.

Sheila does not give the account in chronological order (the order in which it happened). Re-order the facts as you think necessary.

She went to the manager and said if they didn't get rid of the girl, she'd never go there again and would persuade her mother to close their account.

Against her mother's and the assistant's advice she tried a dress on. She looked silly in it. Eva was present because she had brought the dress up from the workroom.

The assistant - Miss Francis - had asked something about it, so the girl held the dress against her to show us what she meant. The dress suited her.

When Sheila tried the dress and knew it was wrong she caught sight of the girl smiling at Miss Francis as if to say 'Doesn't she look awful!'
Sheila was furious and very rude to both of them. Then she went to the manager.

2 There are some details you don't know which you will need to invent for your scene. For instance:
What do her mother and the assistant say about the dress?
What does Miss Francis ask about the dress? What does Eva reply?
What does Sheila say to Miss Francis and Eva when she is being rude?
Decide what you will invent for each of these and for any other questions that occur to you.

3 Refer to the section on Eva Smith on page 34. You will need to know as much as you can about her since she is to be in your scene.

4 In pairs, improvise the scene so that you are aware of how the scene will develop and what the characters will say.

5 Start your scene from the point where Sheila first sees the dress. You are now ready to write the scene. Remember to use phrases from Sheila's account where you can.

Write the scene: Eva goes to Mrs Birling's committee

▷ Write the scene in which Eva goes to Mrs Birling's committee for help.

1 Reread the appropriate incident (pages 40 to 45 of *An Inspector Calls*). Make up the summary of the details given.

2 Rearrange the details if necessary.

3 Invent any details you need.

4 Improvise the scene in groups or pairs. The film version of *An Inspector Calls* added a scene in which Eva visited Mrs Birling's committee. The still from the film (below) may help you.

5 Now you are ready to write your scene.

* Page numbers refer to the Longman Study Texts edition of *An Inspector Calls*.

Write an interview

▷ Imagine that you are a reporter and you have just interviewed one of the characters at the point where the Inspector left them.

1. In pairs or groups draw up a list of questions you would ask your character. On page 33 there are some suggestions to start you off.
2. Organise your questions into a sensible order.
3. Prepare your character's answers. Remember that the answers should be in character, and that there are some things that your character may not wish to admit to unless put under pressure by the interview.
4. Now you are ready to write out your final draft of your interview.

Mr Birling
How responsible do you feel about your part in Eva Smith's death?
If you had your time again, would you alter your behaviour in any way?
Can you afford the public scandal if this case reaches the press?

Mrs Birling
What has been the worst aspect for you about Eva Smith's death?
Is there anything you regret about the way you have brought up your children?

Sheila
What do you think you have learnt from this experience?
Why have you broken off your engagement with Gerald?

Eric
How do you feel about the fact that your father is prepared to cover up your theft?
Why didn't you turn to your parents for help?

Gerald
Do you regret Sheila's breaking off your engagement?
What do you think your parents will say when they hear about this incident?

Eva Smith's diary

▷ Soon after her death, Eva Smith's diary is found. Write her entries relating to the events mentioned in the play in which she was involved.

1 Reread the relevant incidents from the play, and select the facts you will use.

2 We don't know from Eva Smith herself what she felt and thought. But we can make accurate guesses from hints in each of the accounts in these lines:

She'd had a lot to say – far to much – so she had to go.

So that after two months, with no work, no money coming in, and living in lodgings, with no relatives to help her, few friends, lonely, half- starved, she was feeling desperate.

She enjoyed being among pretty clothes.

She felt she was making a good fresh start.

. . . smiling at Miss Francis as if to say: 'Doesn't she look awful?'

She looked young and fresh and charming and altogether out of place down there.

All she wanted was to talk – a little friendliness.

. . . Joe Meggarty's advances had left her rather shaken.

. . . she was desperately hard up and at that moment was actually hungry.

– intensely grateful –

. . . by that time Daisy knew it was coming to an end.

She told me she'd been happier than she'd ever been before.

She kept a rough sort of diary . . .

She was here alone, friendless, almost penniless, desperate. She needed not only money but advice, sympathy, friendliness.

She was claiming elaborate fine feelings and scruples that were simply absurd for a girl in her position.

She didn't want me to marry her. Said I didn't love her – and all that. In a way, she treated me – as if I were a kid.

3 Decide on the basis of your reading what you think Eva Smith felt and thought about each of the people she met. Do you think she felt envious of their wealth? Did she feel unfairly treated by them? What do you think she wanted from life? How powerless did she feel?

4 Reread the play to find out the dates of the events in Eva's life. This will give a clue as to the dates in Eva's diary.

5 Now you are ready to write Eva's diary.

> *For two months now I've had no money coming. I don't know who to turn to. I'm beginning to feel desperate...*

FACTORY OWNER IN SUICIDE SCANDAL

Front page news

▷ Compose the front page newspaper story which tells of the Birling's involvement in Eva's death and Eric's theft.

1. People enjoy reading about apparently respectable wealthy people with a position in a society who fall from their high position. This is the aspect you should bring out in your story. Choose a headline which conveys this. Make the most of the fact that Mr Birling was Lord Mayor, owns a factory and hopes for a knighthood and that the Crofts are a long-established titled family.

2. Emphasise the shocking nature of Eva Smith's death – her pregnancy, her having drunk disinfectant and Gerald's and Eric's involvement in the seamier side of Brumley life.

3. Bring out the irony of Mrs Birling condemning to death her own grandchild.

4. Use features of newspaper style to make your article more authentic:
   Write phrases like '55 year old manufacturer Mr Birling' instead of 'Mr Birling who is in his mid-fifties and owns a factory'.
   Quote the people involved.
   Place adverbs at the beginning of sentences to give an impression of exitement, e. g. 'Yesterday in Brumley the news broke', instead of 'The news broke yesterday in Brumley'.
   Place 'said' at the beginning of a sentence, e. g. 'Said Mrs Birling . . .'.

The play becomes a novel

You have already written versions of Eva's visit to Mrs Birling's committee as a scene from a play, and as an entry in Eva Smith's diary. Now write these versions of the incident: as a short chapter in a novel; and as minutes of the meeting of the Brumley Women's Charity organisation.

1. Consider the different approaches you will need. The minutes will be a purely factual account of what was said, without revealing the emotions of Eva, Mrs Birling or the writer. You can achieve this by using *recorded speech*.

2. A novel will use *direct speech* and will make clear the feelings of the speakers. So a novel will expand the incident, whereas minutes will reduce it. Here is how a novel might deal with Eva's opening words:

   The girl sat down quietly and after some hesitation began. 'I come to your committee because I need your help. My name is Eva Birling – Mrs Birling.'
   'Mrs Birling! What do you mean? This is deliberate impertinence,' exclaimed the cold looking woman who seemed to be chairing the meeting.

Here is how this would be written up in the minutes:

```
The girl asked for help and claimed
that her name was Eva Birling.

Mrs Birling considered this as
deliberate impertinence.
```

Compare the two approaches.

3. Write the chapter in the novel first. Then use it to write your minutes.

An Inspector Calls as theatre

We must not forget that Priestley wrote the play not to be read but to be watched in the theatre. The work in this section asks you to consider it as a play and to consider different aspects of production.

Priestley's advice about writing plays

Read this advice (from *The Art of the Dramatist*) that Priestley gave about writing plays. In groups, discuss how well you think he has followed his own advice in writing *An Inspector Calls*.

J. B. Priestley.

Bring life into the Theatre, the Theatre into life. Think in terms of action, for though plays are mostly dialogue, the talk should be moving towards an action. But be wary of seeing playwriting as story-telling; the techniques are so different, this does more harm than good. Assume that the drama of debate is Shaw's copyright, so don't have people sitting around discussing the atom bomb, unless one of them has an atom bomb and proposes to use it. Try to have a continuous and varied series of little dramas within your big drama; the ability to write like this marks the born dramatist. Always try to make your exposition – that is, the business of giving the audience necessary information – itself dramatic. Cut out all that stuff about ringing for tea and mixing drinks – all the great dead wood of the English Theatre. Try to suggest life going on outside your scenes: in poor, thin plays the characters on the stage seem to be the only people left in the world. Unless you are a religious genius, avoid characters that are almost angels and demons. Aim at a constant slight surprise throughout your scenes, but in your main theme arouse and then satisfy the expectations of the audience. Allow for the audience, which has its own part to play, changing your piece a little; but don't permit too much, for you serve your audience best by being its master.

▷ Write a piece outlining the conclusions of your group discussion.

Staging dramatic moments

Priestley is a master of suspense and surprise. What happens or what is said immediately after each of these speeches which acts as an ironic comment on the speech? What comment is being made?

. . . that a man has to mind his own business and look after himself and his own – and –

No, she didn't exactly go on the streets.

And if you'd take some steps to find this young man and then make sure that he's compelled to confess in public his responsibility – instead of staying here asking quite unnecessary questions – then you really would be doing your duty.

And I tell you that the time will soon come when, if men will not learn that lesson, then they will be taught it in fire and blood and anguish. Good night.

Now look at the pair of them – the famous younger generation who know it all. And they can't even take a joke –

▷ Try acting out one of these dramatic moments. How would you bring out the surprise? Does a pause or silence help? How do the characters look and feel at that moment?

Prepare a production

▷ In groups, choose an important scene and prepare a production of it to be presented to the rest of the class.

1 The scene you choose will depend on the size of your group, but choose one in which a dramatic moment occurs. For instance:

   a) The arrival of the Inspector: 'All right Edna' (page 10) . . .to '*which the Inspector then replaces in his pocket*' (page 12). five parts

   b) Sheila's recognition of her part in Eva Smith's fate: 'Do you know what happened to this girl' (page 18) . . . to '*The other three stare in amazement for a moment*' (page 20). four parts

   c) Gerald's recognition that he is involved: 'That's what I asked myself tonight' (page 23) . . . to end of Act 1 (page 25). three parts

   d) Mrs Birling's realisation that the man she is condemning is her own son: 'Who is to blame then?' (page 45) . . . to end of Act 2 (page 47). five parts, one non-speaking

   e) The Inspector leaves: 'But just remember this' (page 54) . . . to 'it's every man for himself' (page 55). five parts

   f) Gerald and Mr Birling try to let themselves off the hook and fail: 'We can settle that at once' (page 66) . . . to end of play (page 69). five parts

2 Cast your parts and read the scene through a couple of times, until it runs smoothly and you are becoming acquainted with it.

3 Make a list of questions about the situation and the characters' thoughts. For example, if you were working on (f), the end of the play, you might ask:

What does Gerald feel when he says: 'We can settle that at once'?

What is Mr Birling thinking when he says: 'It will look a bit queer, won't it – '?

What are they all thinking when Gerald speaks on the phone?

What should they do when Gerald is phoning?

How should the actors show that this is a moment of great tension?

How should Gerald say: 'This is Mr Gerald Croft – of Crofts Limited'?

How long should Gerald wait before he tells them what he has learnt?

What is each of them thinking when Gerald announces what he's learnt?

How should Gerald say: 'Thanks, I think I could just do with one now'?

How should Sheila say: 'The worst part is'?

How should Birling say: '*You all helped to kill her*'?

How should Sheila say: 'I want to get out of this'?

What is Birling thinking when he says: 'Nonsense!'?

How should Eric say: 'I'm not'?

How can you make it clear to the audience that Eric and Sheila do not share their parents' attitude?

What do Mr and Mrs Birling think about Sheila being, as they put it, hysterical?

What are they all thinking when the phone rings?

How should Mr Birling look when he hears the news?

How should the characters be arranged on stage for the final still picture?

Throughout the scene, what movement should there be?

When you have made your list, decide upon your answers.

4 Decide what props you will need. (Remember that Priestley himself was quite happy if producers wished to dispense with an ordinary realistic set.)

5 Rehearse the scene, bearing in mind your answers to the questions.

6 More questions may come up as you rehearse. Solve them as they occur.

7 Put your scripts away and improvise the scene, using your own words.

This will test your understanding and knowledge of the scene.

8 Learn your words thoroughly. Think about what your character is feeling when he/she says the words and you may find it easier to remember them.

9 Now you are ready to perform your scene to the rest of your class.

Write a theatre programme

▷ Write a theatre programme for a production of *An Inspector Calls*. You should include:

a cover design;

a brief account of Priestley's life;

a summary of the plot of the play and its themes;

a gallery of the characters of the play saying a little about each;

notes on the social attitude and class structure of the period;

a cast list;

a collage of the most important lines in the play.

Here are some questions and suggestions to guide you.

1. Will your cover design show a particular scene from the play? Or will it be an abstract design bringing out a theme, such as police work, or poverty set against riches, or a drawing of Eva Smith? Consider the effectiveness of the cover of the Greenwich Theatre Programme.

2. Select the basic facts about Priestley's life – you will only need to write a paragraph. When was he born? When did he die? What are the most well-known novels and plays that he wrote? What was he like as a person? What themes did he explore in his novels and plays?

3. Bear in mind that your plot summary must be accurate but easy to follow. Audiences have only about five minutes to absorb the information before the play starts. Will you keep the end of the play a secret, or will you hint at it? What do you think is the most important point the play makes?

4. Find photographs of faces from newspapers and magazines which you think best fit the characters. Decide what are the most important characteristics of each character.

5. Use the notes from the 1986 Manchester programme (page 4) to guide you in writing about the historical period. Reduce this information to about a third of the length, by selecting the most important points.

6. Compare the two cast lists on pages 40–41, one from the original production in 1946 and one from a production in 1986. What changes in layout and printing have occurred? Choose actors you know from television and theatre who you think would best suit the parts.

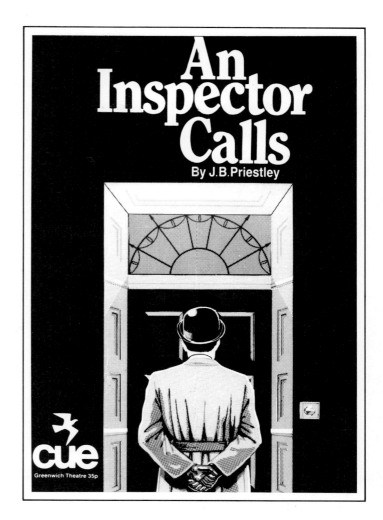

7. Choose about ten quotations which you find particularly important and arrange them on a page in whatever design pleases you. You may add artwork where you think it is helpful.

8. Present your programme as a booklet. The cover design will obviously be on the front page. Look at some theatre programmes and see how they compare with yours. How will you organise the rest of the information? How will you lay it out on the page? Will you break up the print with artwork? It will look more authentic if you can type it.

Dingley's
Oxford Street   Central 8417

FOR BEAUTIFUL FRAGRANT FLOWERS

---

5 points of superiority in the WILLOUGHBY SERVICE
- Good Food
- Fine Wine
- Comfortable Accommodation
- Efficient Service   Scrupulous Cleanliness
- Moderate Charges

4 places in Manchester where these may all be obtained:

THE PRINCES RESTAURANT
Cen. 1979, 5 and 7, Oxford Street

THE PALACE RESTAURANT
Cen. 6048   97, Oxford Street

THE MARBLE STREET GRILL
Marble Street   (Off Mosley Street)

THE GARRICK HOTEL
49, Fountain Street

ALL LICENSED

INCOMPARABLE CHOCOLATE

Is on sale at the Chocolate Stall on the Grand Circle staircase when supplies permit

Cliftons Chocolates Ltd., MANCHESTER

BENNETT & TAYLOR LTD.
Coal and Coke Specialists

5, STANLEY ST., SALFORD
'Phone : BLA 4766

PIANOS and RADIO
BY ALL THE LEADING MAKERS
Crane & Sons Ltd.
202/4 DEANSGATE, MANCHESTER   BLA 5113

MONDAY, 9th SEPTEMBER, 1946, for SIX NIGHTS at 6-30.
Matinee : WEDNESDAY and SATURDAY at 2.

BRITISH PREMIERE.
THE JOINT COUNCIL OF THE NATIONAL THEATRE AND THE OLD VIC IN ASSOCIATION WITH THE ARTS COUNCIL
present
THE OLD VIC THEATRE COMPANY
in
AN INSPECTOR CALLS
A Play in Three Acts by J. B. PRIESTLEY.

Characters in order of appearance :

Arthur Birling	JULIEN MITCHELL
Gerald Croft	HARRY ANDREWS
Sheila Birling	MARGARET LEIGHTON
Sybil Birling	MARIAN SPENCER
Edna	MARJORIE DUNKELS
Eric Birling	ALEC GUINNESS
Inspector Goole	RALPH RICHARDSON

The play produced by BASIL DEAN.

All three acts, which are continuous, take place in the dining-room of the Birling's house in Brumley, an industrial city in the North Midlands.
It is an evening in Spring, 1912.

Scenery and costumes designed by Kathleen Ankers.
Scenery built and painted in The Old Vic Theatre Company's Workshops
Ladies' costumes made in Old Vic Workshops under Morgan Rendell.
Gentlemen's clothes by Morris Angel, 117, Shaftesbury Avenue, W.1.
Wigs by Nathanwigs, 12, Panton Street, S.W.1.
Furniture by the Old Times Furnishing Company.
Electrical Equipment supplied by the Strand Electrical and Engineering Supply Company.
Telephone supplied by the G.P.O.
Cigarettes by Abdulla.

General Manager	For	LAURENCE EVANS
Stage Director	THE OLD	JOHN SULLIVAN
Stage Manager	VIC THEATRE	DIANA BODDINGTON
Assistant Stage Manager	COMPANY	DAVID AYLIFF
General Manager for the Old Vic		GEORGE CHAMBERLAIN

NEXT MONDAY, FOR SIX NIGHTS AT 6-30
Matinee : WEDNESDAY and SATURDAY at 2

THE SADLER'S WELLS BALLET
Monday and Tuesday, Lac des Cygnes (Act. II); Nocturne; Miracle in The Gorbals. Wednesday (Matinee), Lac des Cygnes (Act II); Nocturne; Les Patineurs. Wednesday (Evening), Les Patineurs; Symphonic Variations; Miracle in The Gorbals. Thursday, Les Patineurs; Hamlet; Aurora; Pas de Deux; Dante Sonata. Friday, Les Patineurs; Blue Bird; Pas de Deux; Symphonic Variations; Hamlet. Saturday (Matinee), Lac des Cygnes (Act II); Nocturne; Blue Bird; Pas de Deux; Hamlet. Saturday (Evening), Lac des Cygnes (Act II.); Blue Bird Pas de Deux; Symphonic Variations; Hamlet.
Repertoire subject to alteration.

HAYWARDS
FOR GLASS & CHINA.
FINE DISPLAY OF GLASS IN CUT CRYSTAL
64 & 66 DEANSGATE.   MANCHESTER. 3.

MOTOR

GOOD WORKMANSHIP AND EFFICIENT SERVICE

Circuitt & Hinchliffe, Ltd.
22, Hyde Road, MANCHESTER
'Phone : ARDwick 1690

CENTRAL LAUNDRY
PIQUE DRESS SHIRTS
IRONED BY HAND
CORRECT   FINISH

72, QUAY STREET
Tel. : BLAckfriars 7023

Office Service Bureau
EMPLOYMENT AGENTS FOR OFFICE STAFF COPYING OFFICE

NO FEES CHARGED TO STAFF

TEMPORARY STENOGRAPHERS URGENTLY REQUIRED

30, Cross St.,	71, Lord St.,
Manchester 2.	Liverpool 2.
Tel. BLA 6717/8	Tel. CENTRAL 566

A. LONGWORTH & SONS, LTD
Sanitary Plumbers and Heating Engineers,

146, OLDHAM ROAD MANCHESTER

Telephone : COLlyhurst 1971/2

MONDAY, 23rd SEPTEMBER, FOR TWELVE NIGHTS AT 6-30
Matinee Wednesday and Saturday at 2

ROBERT DONAT
IN TWO NEW PRODUCTIONS
First Week
MUCH ADO ABOUT NOTHING
By William Shakespeare

Second Week
FOR THE FIRST TIME ON ANY STAGE
THE MAN BEHIND THE STATUE
By Peter Ustinov

F. G. RIDE & Co.
Wholesale Electrical Supplies of all kinds

LARGE STOCKS CARRIED

72, GARTSIDE STREET, MANCHESTER

An Inspector Calls
by J B Priestley

The Cast
Arthur Birling — *Russell Enoch*
Gerald Croft — *Steven Mann*
Sheila Birling — *Geraldine Alexander*
Sybil Birling — *Carol Gillies*
Edna — *Flip Webster*
Eric Birling — *Hugh Grant*
Inspector Goole — *Graeme Garden*

Directed by *Richard Wilson*
Set designed by *Saul Radomsky*
Costumes designed by *Stephen Doncaster*
Lighting designed by *Michael Calf*
Sound designed by *Rosalind Elliman*

All three Acts, which are continuous, take place in the dining-room of the Birlings' house in Brumley, a northern industrial city. It is an evening in Spring, 1912.

There will be two intervals of 15 minutes.

The first performance of AN INSPECTOR CALLS at the Royal Exchange Theatre was on Thursday 27 March 1986.

For this production
Stage Manager — *Ann Harrison-Baxter*
Deputy Stage Manager — *Taddy Chamney*
Assistant Stage Manager — *Marcus Holt*
Lighting Operator — *Paul W Jones*
Sound Operator — *Nicky Matthew*
Props Buyer — *David Millard Price*
Master Carpenter — *Rob Stirling*
Set & Props by — *Mike Hubbard, Alan Marshall, Tabby Riley, David Bloodworth*
Assistant Costume Supervisor — *Janet Christmas*
Wardrobe Assistants — *Marie Dunaway, Debbie Attle*
Wardrobe Mistress — *Ann Darlington*
Wig Mistress — *Barbara Taylor*
Wig Assistant — *Jill Sweeney*
Technicians — *Stephen Bedford, Garry White*

Chartered Physiotherapist — *Louise Anderson M.C.F.P.*

Credits
Tobacco supplied by Benson & Hedges
J.N. Nichols (Vimto PLC)
Vimto the Great British drink

Thanks to Ivor Spencer International School for Butler Administration for advice on period etiquette.

This theatre in association with Arden College is part of the Manchester City Council Youth Training Scheme and our participants are:
Amanda Glynn — Workshop
Brent Lees — LX
Malcolm Lisle — Sound
Donna Scully — Publicity

supported by Manchester City Council *and the* District Councils of Greater Manchester.

Reviews of various productions

Read these reviews of various productions of *An Inspector Calls*. With which reviewer do you feel most in sympathy? Which reviewers share your view of the play? Which production would you most like to see? Which actors come closest to your interpretation of the characters?

▷ Look back at the programme you made. Imagine what the production would have been like and write your own review of it.

▷ If you go to see a performance of *An Inspector Calls*, write a review of it.

An Inspector Calls

Opened January 16

BUILT LIKE a well-engineered detective story, the plot of J. B. Priestley's "An Inspector Calls" holds together this somewhat mystical moral tale and makes it all seem credible. Memories of the Old Vic production of 30 years ago, with its starry cast headed by Ralph Richardson, make the present company at the Shaw a trifle underpowered, though James Roose-Evans direction glosses over the weakness.

Bernard Culshaw's setting, consisting mainly of heavy dining-room furniture surrounded by a black void, is remarkably effective in conjuring-up the nouveau-riche atmosphere of the Birlings' home in the industrial north Midlands. At first compact, almost cosy, when the family are gathered to celebrate the engagement of the daughter Sheila to Gerald, a young man higher up in the social scale. But with the arrival of the enigmatic inspector, the setting appears to become as cold as a court-room, each familiar piece of furniture suddenly looking unfriendly.

The guilt-ridden people involved — each one of the five is in some way responsible for the suicide of a local girl — are subjected to intimate questioning by the inspector, a shattering experience which changes their lives. That is, until they realise the 'inspector' was not genuine and that there had been no suicide.

But then Priestley works his clever coup de théâtre — one worthy of Agatha Christie — and we are back at square one, with a difference.

The play still fascinates, and Mr Roose-Evans creates the steadily-increasing feeling of approaching disaster, despite moments such as Eric's bout of hysterics which all but pushes the play over into melodrama.

Douglas Blake

(*Stage 26.1.78*)

EXETER

THE FIRST production under the aegis of **Geoffrey Reeves** the new director of the Northcott is "An Inspector Calls," a choice much in line with his declared policy of providing popular plays.

Produced by **Clive Barker** within an elaborate setting of dark oak, plush and chandeliers designed by **Saul Radomsky**, it is performed not in the broad North Country accent usually associated with the Birling household in Priestley's Yorkshire, but the actors play it out in middle-class-neutral so that the class distinction between the landed gentry of the Croft family and the industrial self-made Birling becomes hardly apparent.

This handling seems to make the suicide of Daisy Renton appear more poignant than in the traditional style of presentation and also has the effect of making **Philip Newman's** portrayal of the master of the house more commanding and nearer to the conventional bore in the eyes of his family than just a voluble parent.

John Collin, poker faced, dry of voice, forceful without being pugnacious makes Inspector Goole a penetrating, yet sombre character whose presence dominates the whole play.

Mary Llewellin as Sybil Birling portrays the stubborn mother with impressive yet gracious command; **Gillian Rhind** gives a bright, clear-cut and sincere performance as the daughter Sheila and **David Griffin** creates an eminently natural character from the easy going son Eric.

(*Stage 18.4.74*)

. . . . . . You feel that the author always calls the tune, that his characters scurry, hither and thither at his bidding, always knowing far less than he does, never in any sort of ambiguous relationship with their creator. It's not something you feel of Chekhov, into whose waters Priestley sometimes sails. For Priestley is most definitely not a subtle ironist and his creatures are pushed down and dusted off without ceremony. We, the audience, are perforce as detached as he is . . . But for all that, *An Inspector Calls* works. It remains, after all, a splendid idea to expose the brisk callousness and the exploitation of the governing class by revealing a family's involvement, as individuals, in the suicide of one of their unnoticed victims, and then to watch them trying to close ranks, as a family, to exonerate themselves.

(Plays & Players Vol 20 '73)

Alan Strachan's production of *An Inspector Calls*, set in 1912 but written in 1945, is a decent, affectionate piece of staging that nonetheless leaves you gasping for air at the plodding obviousness of the play, infuriated by its nudge-nudge coyness of plotting and message, exasperated at its creaking structural carpentry.

(*Financial Times 3–31.12.83*)

THE STAGE

Revival of 'An Inspector Calls'

THE AWFUL awakening that awaits the smug, self-made industrial middle-class in Britain as the result of two world wars is the theme of the fire-and brimstone sermon which Pitlochry Festival Theatre help J. B. Priestley to deliver in their solid realisation of his "An Inspector Calls," introduced to their repertoire on June 12.

Had Priestley written it in 1912, it would have had the virtue of a prophecy; the first production, however, was in 1945, and by setting it in 1912 Priestley profits from a hindsight which allows him to lay bare all the more mercilessly the hypocrisy and meanness of the "I'm all right Jacks" of their time.

The characters are very much at the mercy of his own ruthless shaping of them to fit the purposes of his parable, no less than the mysterious inspector's ruthless exposure of their individual and collective guilt in the death of a poor girl whose first step out of line was to agitate for a wage of 25s instead of 22s 6d a week.

It is a horrifying picture of a society in need of purging, and while director Christopher Denys and his players allow it to stand on its own blunt, full-blooded merits and period, it is impossible not to toy with the idea of an equation with the day of the "lame duck."

Is the solution another cataclysm of blood and anguish, or does hope lie in the more sympathetic attitude of the younger people, Sheila and Eric particularly, who can still feel shame at the cynicism of their elders?

These parts are excellently played by Lois Hantz and Christopher Saul and Donald McIver puts a lot of splendid light and shade into the part of the more worldly Gerald.

But it is in the powerfully realised, vigorous, and accurate performances of Peter Ducrow and Sheila Brownrigg, as the Birling parents, that the true heartlessness of the strata of society Priestley is condemning is fully displayed. Their performances are first-class, and so is Victor Lucas's cutting, telling tempo as the Inspector.

CAST
"AN INSPECTOR CALLS"
Revival of play by J. B. Priestley. Presented by Pitlochry Festival Theatre on June 12. ager. Frederick Krestoff: deputy stage manager. Janet Spearman.
Arthur Birling .... Peter Ducrow
Sybil Birling .... Sheila Bownrigg
Sheila Birling .... Lois Hantz
Eric Birling .... Christopher Saul
Gerald Croft .... Donald MacIver
Edna .... Colette Kelly
Inspector Goole .... Victor Lucas
Directed by Christopher Denys

SWANSEA
'AN INSPECTOR CALLS'

THE WINDSOR Theatre Company's tour of J. B. Priestley's "An Inspector Calls" got off to a highly promising start at the Grand, Swansea. Despite the fact that some of the play's overt political didacticism was played down to cater for today's audiences, it was interesting to note that some of Priestley's targets were still hit dead centre. Indeed, some of the lines have a highly ironic ring today.

Apart from its well-made structure, what audiences seemed also quick to appreciate was the play's balanced, purposeful dialogue. Many young people, for whom this was their first Priestley play, were left arguing strongly about its topicality and the significance of the problems which it poses.

Tony Steedman's bluff portrayal of the commercially successful Arthur Birling was in distinct contrast to the quietly controlled, all-knowing power of Bill Fraser's Inspector Goole. There were interesting and highly contrasted performances also from Carmel McSharry as Sybil Birling, Helen Bourne as her daughter Sheila, Jeffrey Shankley as her son, Eric, and from Anthony Verner as Gerald Croft, Sheila's fiancé. Edna, the maid, was played by Susanna Pope.

The production is beautifully designed and lit and is directed by Hugh Goldie with a sure grasp of the play's qualities.

(*Stage 30.5.74*)

RICHMOND
An Inspector Calls

In an industrial town in the Midlands in 1912, a self-satisfied, well-to-do middle-class family sit down to dinner to celebrate the daughter's engagement. Father was once mayor and looks forward to an imminent inclusion in the Honours List, Mother is busy with charitable works and they all assume that God's in his heaven, all's right with the world.

But the Inspector, calling with news of the suicide of a young girl, throws the spanner into their well-oiled works. This scene makes excellent theatre and the cast, under the taut direction of Ted Craig, never put a foot wrong.

Alfred Marks is ideal casting for the Inspector whose matter-of-factness admirably masks motives. His subtle acting works admirably for the balance of the play.

Peter Vaughan and Adrienna Corri achieve just the right veneer to cover the monstrous people the older Birlings really are, though she looks young enough to be playing the daughter Sheila.

Julie Dawn Cole, Paul Cooper and Christopher Blake are all to be commended in this fascinating revival.

Eric Braun

Some advice for coursework

There are two main types of coursework – the formal essay and the creative piece. In a formal essay, you will be asked to defend your point of view about a particular aspect of the play. In a creative piece you might be asked to write a newspaper article, or an interview, or add another scene. Whichever type you are working on, you must show that you know the play and that your work demonstrates an understanding of the play. This you can do by using the words of the play in your work. This section will help you by giving advice on how to use quotations in both types of coursework.

Using quotations in a formal essay

Here you will be using quotation to support your arguments. Look at these three different ways of using quotation and then read the comments at the top of page 45.

> 1 'Well really! Alderman Meggarty! I must say, we *are* learning something tonight.' This quotation shows that Mrs Birling is ignorant and has a closed mind. She is referring to Gerald who has just said: 'He's a notorious womanizer as well as being one of the worst sots and rogues in Brumley.'

> 2 Mrs Birling reveals her ignorance of what is happening around her and her closed mind when, shocked, she exclaims: 'Well, really! Alderman Meggarty!' on hearing Gerald describe him as a 'notorious womanizer' and a sot and rogue.

> 3 Gerald says about Alderman Meggarty 'He's a notorious womanizer as well as being one of the worst sots and rogues in Brumley.' Mrs Birling is shocked and says: 'Well, really! Alderman Meggarty! I must say, we *are* learning something tonight.'

Number 2 is an example of the best way to use quotation. The writer has used short quotations and weaved them into the flow of her own sentence to make a point about the character of Mrs Birling.

Although number 1 makes the point, it is more clumsy than 2. 'This quotation shows' is awkward, and the quotations are longer than they need be.

Number 3 hardly makes the point at all. The writer is simply telling the tale, saying who said what.

Remember to keep quotations short and frequent and use phrases rather than sentences.

Using quotations in informal work

In a formal essay, you acknowledge the quotation by putting speech marks round it. This would look out of place if, for instance, you were writing the diary of one of the characters.

The same point applies, however: keep quotations short and frequent and use phrases rather than sentences. Look at these two examples and the comments that follows.

An entry from Sheila's diary

> 1 At the time I thought she was very pretty and so could take care of herself. But I knew the Inspector was right when he said that in a kind of way I was jealous of her, and that I'd misused my power as a rich man's daughter. I tried to point out that...

> 2 I told the Inspector she was very pretty and looked as if she could take care of herself. I coudn't be sorry for her. The Inspector said that in a kind of way I might be said to have been jealous of her. I agreed. Then he said I used the power I had, as a daughter of a good customer and also of a man well known in the town, to punish the girl just because she made you feel like that.

Look at the episode on page 23 of the play. You will see that number 1 uses some phrases – 'very pretty', 'could take care of herself', 'in a kind of way', 'jealous', 'power', but has weaved them together in such a way as to show she understands what she has read.

Number 2, however, simply copies the whole passage out without any real thought, and even goes so far as to forget to change 'you' to 'me' at the end.

Longman Study Texts

An Inspector Calls – *J B Priestley*

ISBN 0 582 33205 2

This edition of the play includes a personal essay by Braham Murray who discusses the play through the eyes of a theatre director. In addition, notes and assignment ideas are included.

A selection of plays from Longman Imprint Books and Longman Study Texts:

Longman Imprint Books

Intensive Care edited by Michael Church
Conflicting Generations edited by Michael Marland
John Mortimer Plays
A Special Occasion by Bill Naughton
P'tang, Yang, Kipperbang and Other TV Plays by Jack Rosenthal

Longman Study Texts

Absurd Person Singular by Alan Ayckbourn
Sisterly Feelings by Alan Ayckbourn
The Winslow Boy by Terence Rattigan
Educating Rita by Willy Russell
Equus by Peter Shaffer
The Royal Hunt of the Sun by Peter Shaffer
Macbeth by William Shakespeare
The Merchant of Venice by William Shakespeare
Romeo and Juliet by William Shakespeare
Pygmalion by Bernard Shaw

Titles in the Longman Literature Guidelines series:

Animal Farm
The Diary of Anne Frank
An Inspector Calls
The Winslow Boy
Romeo and Juliet
Macbeth
I'm the King of the Castle

Acknowledgements

We are grateful to the following for permission to reproduce copyright material:

Authors' Agents on behalf of the late Sonia Brownell Orwell and Martin Secker & Warburg Ltd for an extract from *Animal Farm* by George Orwell; Authors' Agents for an extract from *An Inspector Calls* by J. B. Priestley, pubd. Wm Heinemann Ltd; the Author, Alex Robertson for extracts from his article '1912: Arthur Birling's England' *Royal Exchange Theatre Co. Programme*, Manchester 1986; Unwin Hyman Ltd for an extract from *Suffragettes: A Story of Three Women* by Gertrude Coleman; Virago Press Ltd for extracts from *Ordinary Lives* by Carol Adams, © Carol Adams 1982.

We are grateful to the following for permission to reproduce photographs:

BBC Enterprises, pages 28–9; BBC Hulton Picture Library, pages 5, 7, 10 right, 11, 16 right, 21 and 36; Ronald Grant Archives, pages 26 below, 31 and 37; Greenwich Theatre, page 39; Manchester Royal Exchange Theatre, pages 22, 23 below (photo Kevin Cummins), and 41; Mander and Mitchenson Theatre Collection, pages 26 above and 27; Mansell Collection, page 10 left; Museum of London, page 16 left; Old Vic Theatre, page 40; Society for Cultural Relations with the USSR, page 32; John Vickers Archives, pages 2, 14, 23 above, 24 and 29.

Cover illustration by David Brown.

Series designed to Jenny Palmer of Pentaprism.

LONGMAN GROUP UK LIMITED,
Longman House, Burnt Mill, Harlow,
Essex CM20 2JE, England
and Associated Companies throughout the world.

© Longman Group UK Limited 1989
All rights reserved; no part of this publication
may be reproduced, stored in a retrieval system,
or transmitted in any form or by any means, electronic,
mechanical, photocopying, recording, or otherwise,
without either the prior written permission of the
Publishers or a licence permitting restricted copying
issued by the Copyright Licensing Agency Ltd, 33–34
Alfred Place, London WC1E 7DP.

First published 1989

Set in 10½/12½pt Cheltenham Light and 10½/13½ Helvetica Linotron

Produced by Longman Group (F.E.) Ltd.
Printed in Hong Kong.

ISBN 0 582 02178 2